Guard Against Burnout

Seven Proven Keys to Help You Thrive and Flourish in the Dental Field

by
Leslie D. Bower RDH

COPYRIGHT

Copyright ©2017 by Leslie D. Bower
guardagainstburnout@gmail.com

Facebook link: http://fb.me/guardagainstburnout

LinkedIn:https://www.linkedin.com/in/leslie-bower-33b337138/

ALL RIGHTS RESERVED. This book contains material protected under the International and Federal Laws and Treaties. Any unauthorized reprint or use of this material is prohibited. No portion of this book may be reproduced, stored in a retrieval system, or transmitted in any form or by any means- electronic, mechanical, photocopy, recording, scanning, or other- without the express written permission from the author or publisher- except for brief quotation in critical reviews or articles. It is illegal to copy this book, post it to a website, or distribute it by any other means without permission from the authors and publisher.

Leslie D. Bower

Limits of Liability and Disclaimer of Warranty.

The author and publisher shall not be liable for your misuse of this material. This book is for strictly informational and educational purposes.

Disclaimer

The views expressed are those of the author/webmaster and do not reflect the official policy or position of the publisher.

Copyright Use and Public Information

"Scripture quotations taken from the New American Standard Bible® (NASB),
Copyright © 1960, 1962, 1963, 1968, 1971, 1972, 1973, 1975, 1977, 1995 by The Lockman Foundation
Used by permission. www.Lockman.org"

Unless otherwise noted, images have been used with public information laws.

CONTENTS

Dedication	5
Acknowledgements	6
Introduction	7
Key #1: ADAPT	1
Flexibility: How to leave obstacles behind to move into what is possible!	1
Key #2: GENERATE	7
Gratefulness: How to respond in a way the empowers you!	7
Key #3: HONOR	11
How to respect others, keep commitments, and gain confidence!	11
Key #4: EXERCISE	18
Enthusiasm: How to wake up to possibilities!	18
Key #5: CULTIVATE	21
Kindness: How to enlarge your capacity for more fulfilling relationships!	21
Key #6: CELEBRATE	26
Curiosity: How to recapture the heart of childlike wonder and enjoy each season!	26
Key #7: TREASURE	30
Trust: How to build for a lifetime!	30

Dedication

To my Dad and Mom, Ellis (Gus) and Murial (Mac) Gherman. You lived your lives transparently before me, leaving behind a legacy of courage, creativity, and lifelong passion for learning. You overcame great obstacles to discover what God had for you. I am ever grateful!

Acknowledgements

To the Lord Jesus Christ, for apprehending me and lovingly leading me into more truth as my life unfolds.

To those He has chosen for me to walk with in this life, I am grateful for your faithful friendship. Words will not suffice to describe the treasure through relationships that you have extended to me. We have much to rejoice over!

To my fellow dental team members, both past and present, who have been such an encouraging part of my daily life. What a privilege to have been on staff with you!

To my faithful, caring family, who have strengthened and supported me, and encouraged me on while I tried my hand at something new. You never fail to cheer me on!

To Bethany, who has given so much encouragement while editing; and to her family for sharing her with me!

To Jim and Jackie Morey, who have faithfully, enthusiastically, and professionally coached me through this process to completion!

Thank you all!

Introduction

I grew up helping in my Dad's dental office; first as the one who cleaned out the trash and dusted the waiting room, before gradually taking on other responsibilities. By the time I was in high school, I could competently assist my Dad in most situations.

When I was finishing up high school, dental hygiene began to be recognized as a vital part of the dental team. My Dad and others in the area worked diligently to establish a dental hygiene program at the local junior college. I was accepted in the 3rd class from that school, graduating in 1974. While I was in school, a law was passed in Washington State to allow a dental hygienist to perform more functions. When I graduated, I applied for a position that included practicing these expanded duties.

It was a busy time where I faced jumping out of our controlled safe school environment into the real world. As much as my instructors had tried to prepare me, I still recall the early days of my practice in hygiene with a sense of anxiety. Previously, I had been a dental assistant so I thought I was somewhat prepared for this leap.

What I was not prepared for was the constant nagging pressure and tension of maintaining the best interests of the patient, doing a proficient job, staying on time, relating with the other team members, and physical pain of repetitive motion. Along with these issues, most patients were wary of me cleaning their teeth. In the geographical area that I resided, the concept of a hygienist cleaning your teeth was novel to many patients coming in.

I was on the road to burnout.

While training in dental hygiene, I had no idea that the most important skills would not be in the process of sterilization and keeping a clean field, the examination and diagnosis of the patient's dental health, the techniques of instrumentation, or innumerable other practices specific to the field of dentistry, **BUT in the diagnosing of my own state correctly and the practice of these keys to better serve the patient and be a team player.**

These seven keys for a fulfilled and thriving life that I would like to share with you find their roots in God's nature of Love. Since He created me, I have confidence in His instructions on how to go forward into success.

Although I am in great need of practice, *I find that when I choose to apply these keys to both my personal and professional life, I am able to guard against burnout and move forward confidently.*

First, each solution must be applied to my **thoughts**. I take responsibility to evaluate my thoughts and align them with the key concept.

Then it takes further **action** on my part to bring the keys to life. As I consistently practice these keys, they will become **habits**.

These key habits lead to a **lifestyle**.

In my experience, these keys unlock immense opportunity to thrive and flourish in the midst of life's unfolding challenges.

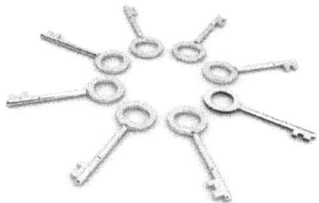

Key #1: ADAPT

Flexibility: How to leave obstacles behind to move into what is possible!

Would you like to be able to grow and progress through each situation you find yourself in? Would you prefer to thrive and not just survive?

I grew up with certain expectations based on the training I received from my parents and my observations of others' lives. By the time I was a young adult, I had a plan in place and was working on accomplishing it. I expected to finish school, get married, have a family and career and enjoy all of this! These are good hopes and dreams. Somewhere along the way, I had to come to grips with things not turning out just the way I had planned. I had to become flexible.

Unmet expectations- just the beginning

We got off the bus in Athens, Greece in front of a small hotel on a dark quiet street. Crossing the lobby and entering into the elevator, our tour group split up to find our assigned rooms.

My roommate was acquainted with others on the trip and after surveying our room, went to visit a friend. The hotel was undergoing some renovation and part of the rooms were redecorated with a new color scheme. This friend's room was located in a recently renovated area.

Ours was not. My friend went to ask for a relocation to a newly renovated room.

While this was going on, I opened the drapes to reveal a breathtaking vista. Our view from this side of the hotel was of the world-renowned Acropolis illuminated in the darkness.

We ended up transferring to a newly renovated room which had a delightful view of the street and other hotels.

Sometime later, when I overheard my roommate's reflection on this event, her version did not include the differing views outside, but focused on the differing layout and color scheme. She felt that we were missing out because we had been stuck in one of the older rooms. She was satisfied when she had a room like the other travelers.

In my life, I have the constant tug between these two rooms. In both rooms, I have everything I need to have a comfortable stay. In both rooms, I have a view. One room is just like what the others have. The thing that sets the one room apart from the other is the scope of the view. How I can let go of the familiar to embrace a different view?

My dear friend was discussing an upcoming event where we were both going to be speaking to a group of women. In the conversation, she expressed several times that she looked to others and wished that she had a relationship with God like she thought they did. She struggled with her relationship and she felt like she wasn't measuring up.

We explored this and began to see the two-room pattern. We could see that this was hampering her. She was basing her **expectation** of what her relationship with God should look like by what she thought mine was. We realized that she was comparing. She felt lacking and this was discouraging to her. We ended up laughing about this most common human phenomenon!

I have seen this pattern in my own life many times. I can make a plan based on the pattern that I see played out around me. I put on skills to equip me to succeed in that area.

I go forward with my plan and then something happens that I hadn't counted on. An obstacle appears. It doesn't fit the pattern I had in my mind. I begin to compare my **expected** result to what is in my path.

This is the critical point of choice for me. Depending on my choice there will be two different outcomes. I can stay in my unmet expectations.

Although I can still see what I wanted, I am not going to be able to reach my intended plan. It feels like options have dried up. I begin to rehearse the reasons for my choice in my head. I hunker down to make do.

The emotional markers of this are fear of failure, discouragement, helplessness, anger, and self-pity. I have chosen to become a victim of my circumstances. In my experience, this path becomes a dead end.

Or I can work through the disappointment and disorientation to see what is **possible** from here.

In order to make this choice, I will have to face fear again. This doesn't look like what I expected. I will have to go where I've not gone before; I will have to go outside my preparation and experience so far. It will not be familiar.

If I choose this path, I can feel the fear, but I can also see a different view. My vista is enlarged. As I survey the situation, I'm looking for the possibilities from here. My heart is encouraged. Hope begins to arise!

A number of years ago, I was blessed to spend a holiday with dear friends in England.

As we drove to various destinations, I kept seeing the sign "Give Way". This is the English version of "Yield".

Many times, in the country side, this sign would show up at a crossroads where there were several choices of direction. The way forward would be obscured by tall shrubbery that is commonly used along the edge to give privacy to the homes near the roadway.

I felt God speaking to me about this. Give way. In my walk through this life, I will continually have this choice before me. There is a way to yield and still pursue my heart's desires begins with giving up my insistence that it must look the way I originally envisioned.

The original "Yield" sign in my life happened when I was apprehended by the Lord Jesus.

From that day forward, I have been on a journey full of discovery designed by Him with me as an active participant. In the Bible, I discovered that He had promised to plant good and fulfilling desires in my heart.

As I learned about His principles for living life, I began the process of aligning my choices with His Word. His faithfulness to me cannot be measured, but I can say that in this journey, I have had many opportunities to yield my expectation to have, look, be and do like everyone else in order to have Him open up the vistas of His higher and better plans and ways to me.

I have discovered two opposing words that bring this concept into focus for me. I think of it as two sides of the same coin.

Scarcity

- Based on **unmet expectations**
- Leads to discouragement
- Stuck, angry, look to blame
- Loss of motivation
- Lack of creativity
- Isolation, burnout
- Winter, atrophy

Abundance

- based on **yielded expectations**
- Leads to peace
- Reaching out, exploration
- Increased possibility
- Solutions not seen before emerge
- Hope, integrated with others
- Grow, thrive

When I begin to struggle with the emotions of discouragement and self-pity, I look for the source. Then the choice looms before me once again

If I'm on my game, I actively make the choice to be grateful for the obstacles and start looking for the possibilities in the situation

If I'm off my game, this process may take longer. That's ok. I'm in this for a lifetime!

You may be saying to yourself, "why would this matter in my job?"

In the dental field, I have daily opportunity to train in being quick to adapt! With an ever-changing schedule, unexpected needs that must be met, people issues, equipment malfunction, the best laid plans are unfolding and reemerging as the day goes on.

Have I chosen to be stuck in my **unmet expectations**? What if I gear up for whatever is **possible**? It will show up wherever I go that day. Each of us has a vital component to bring into the atmosphere around us. I want to bring the abundant side of the coin!

Application:

How have you been affected by the choice of another person to stay stuck in unmet expectations?

How have you been affected by someone making the choice to switch into possibility thinking?

When you are with someone, which state affects you the most?

Choose an area of your life. How do you see your outlook affecting the outcome?

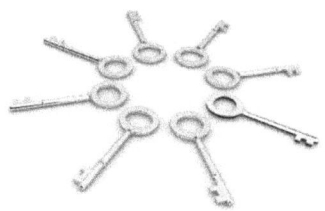

Key #2: GENERATE

Gratefulness: How to respond in a way the empowers you!

After a particularly challenging and fun-filled week at a retreat center in the mountains outside of Atlanta, I had a chance to practice my choice to be grateful.

Several of us were being transported to the airport in the early morning hours to catch our flights. As we waited in the dark for the shuttle to come, we began to discuss the tight schedule. It became apparent that some of us would not make our flights as planned. Anxiety and fear began to assail me.

I had the earliest flight out and the airport was known for the long line at security. Someone asked me how I was doing and I expressed my concern. At the same time, the lights of the shuttle appeared over the hill. We all got on as quickly as possible. As we headed out, the driver apologized for the inconvenience and explained that her GPS had not been working. In the darkness, she had missed a turn.

When we settled in for the 1 1/2-hour drive ahead of us, a gentleman put forth a solution to get as many on flights as possible. "Let's focus on getting the earliest ones off and running as we pull in," he suggested. Soon everyone was busy strategizing. When we pulled into the airport, we worked as a team. One fellow ran with me and directed me to the airline desk. "Tell them your story," he said, as he ran on.

I pulled my gear up to the desk, put down my ticket and identification and explained that our shuttle driver had gotten lost in the dark without the help of her GPS, putting me behind by 40 minutes. The staff at the desk listened to my explanation with professional courtesy. As I shared the poor shuttle driver had tried her best, I saw their eyes change.

One quickly took my carryon and checked it, and explained that I would have to make a run for it. Printing out my ticket, the other one came from behind the desk and asked me to follow her. We went through a door and she took me down the hallway, ushering me through a security checkpoint with no line.

I arrived at my cross-country flight as most of boarding was completed. The staff at the first desk had called ahead and I was greeted with kindness by the flight attendant.

As I got settled in my seat, I looked back at this experience with amazement. Several thoughts went through my head. It was clear to me that I would have missed my flight without the willing help of my fellow travelers and the airline staff. Their experience being applied to my plight changed the outcome. At each potential roadblock, there were those who helped me progress.

The fuel that keeps me going forward is exercising my choice to be grateful.

The writer Paul states," Rejoice in the Lord always; again, I will say, rejoice! Let your forbearing spirit be known to all men. The Lord is near. Be anxious for nothing, but in everything by prayer and supplication with thanksgiving let your requests be made known to God. And the peace of God, which surpasses all comprehension, shall guard your hearts and your minds in Christ Jesus." Philippians 4:4-7 NASB

Each time life doesn't go according to my plan; I have the opportunity to put these words into practice.

On the way to the airport, I used gratefulness in two ways. I grounded myself in the present by thanking God for His plan for me, and while acknowledging that my plan wasn't working and surrendering to what was next, I left the past behind.

I was then poised to begin again and not waste time in what-if or who's to blame. I effectively cut off those two opponents. I mastered fear and condemnation, seeing them as thought patterns that drain away my capacity to make forward movement. I used a grateful response as a weapon against those thoughts, refusing to go into that ineffective cycle.

The second way I used gratefulness was as a posture, leaning forward to see what could be next, which put me in a receptive mode. I was poised for action. I could be directed.

When I start my day in a grateful stance, thanking the Lord for His plan in my life, I am also sowing into the future. I am aligning myself with His promise.

I'm like a soldier-in-training on the ground, while He sees everything from beginning to end. I can gain in this area every time I habitually train and expand my capacity. In this way, when the crisis comes, I have that capacity to fall back on.

Each situation holds the promise of opportunity to hone my skill at this. Right now, I weight train with a delightful coach who reminds me that perfection is not the goal; excellence is.

When I first start a new routine, it seems awkward and slow. I have to constantly think about my actions. I add one thing to the next. As mastery begins to happen, my routine becomes more fluid, more natural.

I recall having a fellow hygienist who was a master at giving "thanks". While I was a beginner, I watched her as she interacted with others. I looked forward to seeing her at work. She effectively changed the atmosphere as she acknowledged how others were enriching her life by the things that were in their job description or by being there as a patient. She could have taken it for granted. By not doing this, she encouraged us all.

Have you ever been in a situation where someone was expressing anger inappropriately?

I have been both the one expressing the anger and the one receiving the anger. It's not fun! While stuck in anger, no forward progress occurs. When I choose ungrateful, I'm left on my own, stuck in a dead end.

When I choose a grateful response, God is near. I am able to draw near to Him I can bring about a change in the spiritual atmosphere by this one strategy. Gratefulness disarms my fear and anger, and it gives a place for true solutions to emerge. Then the creative ideas start popping up! Do I do this perfectly? Not on your life! Am I training in it? You bet! I like the results I get when I choose to be grateful.

Application:

When did you last feel grateful towards someone else?

When did you last find yourself in a circumstance that was discouraging for you?

How have you pushed through a difficult situation by generating gratefulness?

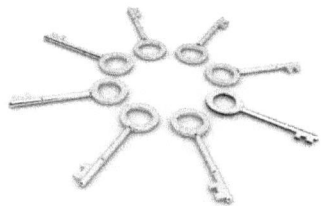

Key #3: HONOR

How to respect others, keep commitments, and gain confidence!

"Finally, brethren, whatever is true, whatever is honorable, whatever is right, whatever is pure, whatever is lovely, whatever is of good repute, if there is any excellence and if anything worthy of praise, let your minds dwell on these things." Philippians 4:8 NASB
This key strategy opens my heart to care for others, to find solutions to problems, and to gain courage. What attribute or quality can I find to honor about each person or situation that I encounter?

Honor Each Person

As we took advantage of the fresh spring day and walked around the downtown area of the city, my friend and I were chatting away, using our time to catch up with each other. Approaching us was what appeared to be a homeless person pushing a shopping cart. His eyes were downcast. My friend took a few moments to look forward and call out a cheery hello adding a question, "Doesn't this beautiful sunshine make a difference?"

The person looked up and flashed an appreciative smile as we passed each other. It was a small act of courtesy that conveyed honor. The atmosphere changed for us three in that moment.

Effectively listening

I recently had a surgical procedure done. My physician referred me to the surgeon. When I went for the prior exam and consult, I was nervous, apprehensive, and felt very vulnerable.

I knew that the surgeon was on a tight schedule. I expected a short brusque professional 10-minute appointment.

I was not prepared for a person to quietly sit down, maintain eye contact and ask me how I was doing. It was disarming. He created a space for me to express my concerns.

He empathized with me, encouraged me and discussed options, providing appropriate information. He conveyed to me that he was here to serve me with my best in mind. My time with the surgeon that day was 20 minutes. I left feeling honored and respected.

Even though I was still apprehensive about the actual day of surgery, I trusted the surgeon to treat me with dignity and keep my best interests in mind.

How did he accomplish this shift in my thinking towards him in such a short time?

I think it was because he chose to engage me as a person. He focused on my concerns as important. He conveyed his desire to bring the best solution to my problem that he could. I call this 'staying in **the now**."

Short-circuit

Recently, I had a friend over for dinner, a game and a movie to celebrate her birthday. While we were playing the game, she was taking staged photos, connecting on social media and posting. During our last minutes before her departure, she caught a ding on her phone and interrupting the flow of conversation, she answered the post and began to show me what she had been following during the evening. It left a sadness in my heart. I felt jerked from place to place. I can recall times when I was doing the same thing.

Staying in **the now** requires me to know the person I am with in that person's current state.

What impression was left last time by our interaction? Did things end on a positive note? Were there intense moments or disconnects that colored the person's or my perceptions?

When I choose to begin in **the now**, I give space for the other person and myself to create something new.

Another aspect of being in **the now** is to leave the past hour behind with its wins and losses, its uncomfortable moments, its questions, and move forward unhindered by the past.

I have the privilege to work in a patient oriented office. From greeting the patient in the waiting room to returning them to the front office desk, we want to serve that person.

Make room

A new patient came into the office because of a painful toothache. He had been to ER over the weekend and now was forced by the circumstance to finally come into the dental office. The Doctor asked me to perform part of the periodontal screening.

As I entered the room to meet him, the wave of fear coming towards me was almost visible. Furthermore, he was embarrassed because the fear had kept him from managing his dental needs.

My first action was to thank him for choosing us to help him in this very stressful time. I continued by asking him if he had been apprehensive about this visit.

I gave him room to express his fears and concerns, and did the best I could to give appropriate information and encouragement. I explained what my part could be to help him move towards a healthier condition.

This first visit resulted in a gradual building of relationship where together as a staff, we were able to help this man disarm his fear of the dentist and establish a healthier condition in his mouth. Though each visit he made was a continuation of the journey, we emphasized his progress and what would be accomplished in our current time together.

After I interacted with the fearful person, I moved on to the next appointment. I shifted gears and left the stress of the previous situation behind, focusing on the next patient.

At the end of the day, I want to know that I gave my best to each person I interacted with. This keeps me from being bogged down.

If I stay with each person, I gain opportunities that I would have missed if I went off in other directions in my mind.

Honor Commitments to Time

In our culture, keeping an appointment with another person is seen as honoring. Being on time denotes that I value what is to occur and the person or people that I'm meeting. The practice of this small habit reaps big dividends.

Running late

The patient was late for the appointment due to unforeseen circumstances. As I seated her, I accepted her apology, and reassured her that I understood. I thanked her for coming. Then I explained the commitment I had to my next patient and told her what I would be able to accomplish for her in the remaining time. We made a plan for her next visit to include what could not be completed that day. She expressed gratefulness for this plan.

Some of the most trying days for me as a health care provider are when I find myself running behind schedule. Then I am the one apologizing to the patient.

Because of this, our team makes great effort to work together. We decided to care for each other. We help each other with the duties that we are trained for. We keep an eye out for unforeseen circumstances that are threatening to derail our schedule. We do what we can to support each other. How can I help my coworker get back on time? Whatever that takes, I'm doing it!

Honor My Word to Others

As a young girl, I remember my Mother holding me accountable for my commitment to have a friend over for the afternoon. We had made plans some time earlier, but as the day approached, another opportunity opened up for me. I was invited to a party that I knew didn't include my friend. I wanted to be two places at one time.

I was tempted to call and reschedule, giving some excuse for the change. My Mom weighed in on this plan, saying that I had given my word and she expected me to honor it and honor the friend I had looked forward to seeing.

As it turned out, this friend told me that she knew I had been invited to the party, and had expected a phone call. She expressed how valued she felt by my choice to keep to our plan. We ended up having a delightful afternoon that led to a deepened friendship.

Honor My Word to Myself

I find that keeping my word to myself is the biggest challenge. When I begin each day, I have a choice to follow through with the plans I have made for that day. The difficulty arises when I have to say no to something or someone because I have a prior commitment to myself. What can help me when I find myself doing this?

Let me share a simple example.

Especially around holidays, all kinds of delicious food seem to show up in our staff breakroom. During one season, I had made a goal to establish healthy nutritional choices. I wanted to stay on track, but I also wanted to eat that special confection! Help! I was wrestling with the conflict within! What will win out? How can I find the wherewithal to stick with my course?

Go to the **why!**

Why did I make the goal? What is the goal based on?

If I can clarify and strengthen **why** I am making the choice, I will be able to acknowledge the kindness of the one bringing the treat in to share, yet stick to my long-term choice for myself.

In order to set myself up for success in keeping my word to myself, I have found that setting a time of completion for the commitment helps me focus and gives me a target. I can deflect distraction because I know there will be a time of completion. Afterwards, I can relax and rejuvenate.

I endeavor to set realistic goals with a little wiggle room. Then I can renegotiate with myself and still hit the target.

One of the best strategies that I have been introduced to is to share my goal with those around me and ask for their support. I still carry the major weight to accomplish what I say I am committed to, but words of encouragement and evaluation are vital!

There are times when one commitment will win out against another just because of the **why** behind it. When a request is made, I can then weigh the one **why** against the other **why** and possibly renegotiate my agreement.

Some commitments are non-negotiable. I must say no at any cost. My integrity as a person depends on it. For me, these find their basis in the Bible, the revealed Word of God.

Honor God

When I go to the deepest layer of honor, I recognize that my foundation has come from God, my Creator, and therefore He is the expert on what is best for me.

God keeps His Word to Himself.

He keeps His Word to His creation.

He keeps his Word for all of time.

I have a belief system that has at its core the promise that God has a master plan for my life and I am on a pathway of discovering what it is. I want to honor Him in my thoughts, words and actions. I want to do my best to stay alert and keep to the path!

Application:

When did I last feel that someone honored me?

How did I benefit from this?

When did I consciously choose to honor another person?

What does my track record show about how I honor commitments to myself?

Who could I trust to support and encourage me to take steps forward?

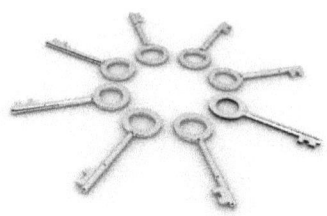

Key #4: EXERCISE

Enthusiasm: How to wake up to possibilities!

Weight training is one example of exercise. The goal of weight training is to gain and maintain muscle. To build muscle, I must push through to a place of discomfort. If I press through this discomfort by a few repetitions, then the muscles involved will increase in strength for the next time.

This is the pathway to growth. My limit must be tested and then surpassed in order to gain more muscle tissue.

When I exercise enthusiasm, I choose to be present and enjoy what is before me.

Focus on the good

While we were sitting around the table, our boss asked us this question, "who is your favorite patient and why?' As we each shared about a person who came to mind, others were quick to chime in with reasons they also enjoyed seeing this person. . When we read their name on the schedule, we looked forward to seeing them.

Everyone had a difficult time choosing just one person! We wanted to linger and rehearse the special moments with people that had touched our lives

Characteristic of the remembrances was the theme of a person who came in upbeat and encouraging. We went on with the time refreshed and encouraged. We had focused on the others' goodness.

Avoid negativity

While my neighbor and I were discussing the recent break in and robbery of a house nearby, I began to remember other times when I had been in this position. I shared about the time I was broken into and coming upon the scene a few minutes later. Soon my neighbor added a story along the same lines. We both began to have feelings of vulnerability and fear. Then she wisely said, "but that is all in the past and we were taken care of."

Our focus had led us down a path that added nothing encouraging to our day. When she changed the focus, we were off in a more positive direction. Soon, our spirits were lifted.

I can't control all the different things and events that will come my way, but I can choose my response. In this way, I can steer clear of that which would rob me of momentum.

Allow for miscalculations

Several years ago, I was invited to be part of a team who were creating an event that would unfold over several days ending on New Year's Day. The purpose of the event was to showcase what a culture of honor could accomplish.

We spent several months as a team planning each part of the event. We secured a location in the beautiful Cascade Mountains. We researched and tested our plans on a smaller scale. We tried to think of possible variables and created a contingency plan for each one of these.

As the days unfolded, all was going according to plan. We were building great momentum towards the last celebratory evening and morning. Then a severe drop in temperature occurred.

The plans we had made to keep the facility warm were not able to keep up with the cold temperatures. We gathered together to assess the situation. The pressure increased as each one brought forth how that could affect the outcome of our celebration.

Then one person chimed in with a tentative solution to one facet of the plan. While we were mulling this idea over, someone responded with enthusiasm. I watched as the tension broke and the atmosphere shifted among us.

We went onto overcome every obstacle. The celebration was all the more precious because of the tenacity we had exercised in order to apprehend it!

Have patience with those who struggle

For whatever reason, some people I encounter are unable to be enthusiastic. That's ok. I can extend kindness and understanding to those who find themselves in seasons of puzzlement, grief or loss. Doing so may open a door for encouraging them.

Exercising enthusiasm about what is ahead gives me an edge. I can look at the future and smile! Enthusiasm has a way of becoming contagious!

Application:

When was the last time you remember being encouraged by someone else's enthusiastic demeanor?

What recent event caught you off guard? What was your initial response?

What situation or place could you be the one bringing enthusiasm to change the atmosphere?

How would that benefit others? How would that benefit you?

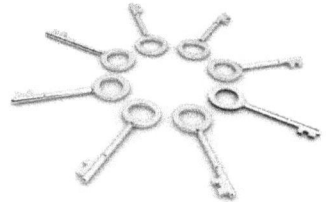

Key #5: CULTIVATE

Kindness: How to enlarge your capacity for more fulfilling relationships!

"Do not let kindness and truth leave you;" Proverbs 3:3 NASB

"Please don't judge me."

When the patient entered the room, she was barely able to sit down. Her anxiety level was very high. As she sat down, she said, "Please don't judge me." I was taken back by her comment. I quickly reassured her that I would be on her team to bring her relief from whatever her need was at that visit. How could I best accomplish this? We began the exam and it became clear that she had neglected her dental health for some years. She was ashamed of this. With as much gentleness as I could convey, I reassured her that she was here now, and we would go forward from here. I held out kindness to her. She visibly relaxed. Over the course of several visits, she honored me with her story of how she became so afraid of the dentist.

Many people will think this in their mind and not say it, "please don't condemn me."

I have become aware that I am continually making assessments about people and situations around me. This is like a built-in radar system. I have found that I base much of my response to another based on that person's posture, facial expression, clothing, age, gender, and the list goes on. This is second nature to me.

What will I do with all that information?

Therein lies the challenge. Beyond wise responses to an immediate threat, I have much choice in this matter.

I can be active in choosing to be kind, extending goodwill towards each person I come in contact with. I can keep the door for effective communication open between us.

My friend introduced me to a man who was a very accomplished entrepreneur and computer specialist. As she introduced me to this man, she said, "Leslie is a dental hygienist." I saw an immediate reaction as the man stiffened and replied, "you're the one who is always making me feel like I'm six years old and in trouble again."

Even though we both laughed, a very real barrier was there between us. I hastened to find some other direction for the conversation to go, but the damage had been done.

Somewhere in his experience with a hygienist, I suspect he felt that he had been cornered. He was told truth, but kindness had been left out. Perhaps he felt that he was not respected.

It is such a delicate balancing act between being kind and being truthful. I have come to the conviction that it is a kind act to bring truth into each relationship.

Reflecting on my own journey, I see times where I was receptive to someone bringing a differing view. At times this was a painful process. If I knew the person cared about me, I was more receptive to the truth being brought to my attention.

When I first graduated from training, I was very zealous about making sure that the person heard all that I was evaluating and understood the ramifications of periodontal disease, the potential loss of health and teeth. I gave extended instruction on homecare and critiqued the patient's performance.

I felt that this was fulfilling my responsibility to the patient. Many times, I imagine that the person felt overwhelmed by what I was telling them.

In my efforts to educate the patient on the effects of periodontal disease, I forgot to be kind. How does one best receive information? Did they feel that they were heard? Did they feel somewhat bullied?

Now I look for the right moment; the teachable moment. It varies from patient to patient. When I hit on the right combination, you can see the light dawn for the patient.

The foundation of trust is a good place to start. Once the person can see that I am there to honor and serve him, I then can bring the benefit of addressing his needs in a way that shows kindness and respect for him. I am there to support him in what he decides are his priorities.

Kindness is characterized by putting the other person first in the exchange.

I like to think of how I would feel in that person's place. How would I respond to what is being presented?

When I first began to practice sharing about dental health and how to maintain it with patients, I heard this over and over, "No one ever told me this before!" I was shocked! How could someone practice with integrity and not educate the patient?

Then I began to see a trend. When that patient would return for a checkup, and I would update them on their dental health status, they would say, "no one has ever **told** me this before!"

What was going on? I knew that I had covered this as part of their previous exam.

I talked to the other hygienists that I was acquainted with. We had each experienced a similar dilemma. I remember that moment when I got it.

The patient was really relaying to me, "I have never **heard** this before!" That is a different challenge.

The atmosphere that words are spoken in is crucial. The context that disarms fear and anxiety contributes to someone being able to actually process the information being given them.

I think back to my appointment with the specialist. I was feeling vulnerable, fearful, and ignorant about my own condition. The surgeon wisely set a context which included respect, honor, kindness and then information.

I know for myself, I can tell if I have really heard the truth about some area of my life. My choices will reflect if I have been able to hear the reality of my situation. My behavior will change. I will go from point A to point B.

With any change, there is a certain amount of resistance to overcome. How badly do I want the prize?

I go from compliance to enrollment. I go from "you take care of me; I'm doing this because you say I need it" to "I want to have this result; what do you recommend I do to achieve this?"

It's almost like something new gets created. If I want it bad enough, I will seek out a way to get there.

When this happens for a patient, that person is choosing a course of action in order to get the result he wants. I get to be in a position to support him!

When endeavoring to cultivate kindness, I think the crux of the matter is in the statement that Jesus made,

"You shall love the Lord you God with all your heart, and with all your soul, and with all your mind." This is the great and foremost commandment. And a second one is like it, "You shall love your neighbor as yourself." Matthew 22:37-39

Application:

Think of a time when you felt valued. What were the actions that contributed to this?

Think of a time when you extended good will to another person. What were you thinking about?

How do you want to be treated? What constitutes safety and comfort for you? What do you need in order to go forward?

What small action could you incorporate to extend kindness to another during this next week?

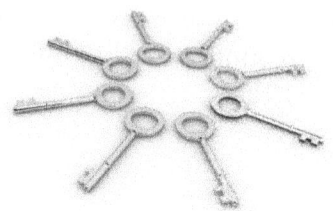

Key #6: CELEBRATE

Curiosity: How to recapture the heart of childlike wonder and enjoy each season!

I look forward to every Monday. It is the day set aside for my grandchildren! These precious ones come in different sizes, colors, genders, and personalities. As they burst through the door, a sort of organized bedlam occurs! They bring with them shoes, coats, bags full an odd assortment of essentials and treasures. They don't just arrive; they invade and scatter love and enthusiasm throughout my whole house, making it a home!

Have you ever noticed how alive with questions children are?

These include the big five: What, When, Where, How and Why! It is a good wake-up call for me. As I stay in the moment with them, we can go on journeys together; delightful romps both backwards and forwards and even sideways! The regular routine becomes a small adventure.

What would it take for me to experience this as I go along through the whole week? I know there must be a schedule and a plan to accomplish duties assigned there-in.

Yet I know that the small unexpected variances can bring needed color and sparkle that brighten and expand one's outlook.

Why not vary it?

Once while listening to someone I admired as an innovator, I heard him state that he challenged himself to change one thing in his routine each day. The examples he gave ranged from small changes like trying out a new flavor in his coffee or driving a different route to work to taking on a large project that he had avoided because of the unknown scope of what was involved.

Was I flexible enough to do this? Since then, I have gained much encouragement to practice this. Even small seemingly insignificant changes have led to a richer and more satisfying day to day experience.

In order to be curious, I find that I need to upset my automatic reset to stay in the familiar. I have a granddaughter who has always pushed the limits of the familiar. She was up and walking with speed at 9 months. She is full of energy and life, putting on new skills each day. I would like to emulate her strategy of constant exploration.

Enjoy the differences

One area that is rich for exploration, is the discovery of other human beings.

While gaining some business training, I was exposed to a wonderful and entertaining discovery journey. It involved an exercise where the moderator listed common human characteristics of thinking and outlook, loosely divided in to four categories. He asked us to make a decision based on what we had just heard to join one of the four groups.

He then asked each group to list the top ten characteristics of that group in order of importance when relating to others. Many earnest voices filled the room. A spokesman was asked to share from each group while the other three groups listened. As each spokesman shared, much laughter filled the room.

It was amazing how clearly in just a few minutes each group had assembled a list that characterized how they saw the same issues. As each spokesman shared, faces came into my mind. I saw how interaction with others could be become a discovery process instead of a butting heads event.

How does it work, this discovery of another person? In my experience, I see it starting with observation and then listening to the other person.

What does it feel like when I think I am being listened to?

I feel respected. I may gain security. I am open to trusting the person who is interested in hearing what I have to say. I feel included. I am more likely to open up to the person who is treating me respectfully by showing that interest.

I made a commitment to myself to practice looking for the delightful differences in the people that came into my path. With a foundation of gratefulness and honor, it is a delightful journey to begin!

From time to time, I am brought up short by a situation to evaluate myself.

If I am dissatisfied with how a relationship has unfolded, what could I do to improve the interactions taking place?

I find that asking myself these questions can be a helpful place to begin.

What has been established? Is the person more open or more closed than when we began? Did the person and I have open clear communication about what was involved?

Is that due to action or inaction on my part? Did I deliver what I promised?

Can I give the person opportunity to answer these questions?

I find it helpful to ask others as well. Friends or colleagues can give me a more accurate picture of what I convey that is past my one-sided viewpoint.

Being open to the feedback from another person is a step into the unknown where the truly curious get to go!

What kind of listener am I? How well do I practice this? Do I keep appropriate eye contact? Am I observing the other person's demeanor, posture, and tone of voice? What is my demeanor, posture and response conveying?

Am I formulating my response as he is speaking? Have I already decided on a course of action? Am I somewhere else entirely in my mind?

So many questions! This is the essence of celebrating curiosity. Change will come. I want to be in a position to explore it!

Application:

What area have I always been drawn to but not ventured into yet?

What small step towards that area could I take this week?

What current relationship would I like to see expand or improve?

How could I begin the conversation to do that? When will I begin?

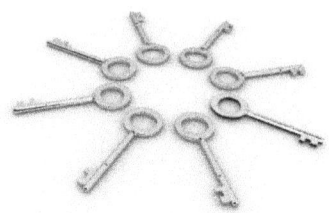

Key #7: TREASURE

Trust: How to build for a lifetime!

How is trust built? What makes me trust another person?

One way to think of trust as a bank account. In a bank account, there are basically three functions: deposits are made contributing to a balance; interest is gained on the safeguarded balance, and withdrawals are made. As long as the account is not overdrawn, it remains in good standing.

When a relationship begins with another person, the ground rules are explored and agreed upon. One common area that agreement must be reached is the use of time. As I make an appointment with one of our patients, we explore options that are usually 3-6 months away. We discuss the way in which a change of plans can be made.

We have built in a way for each of us to renegotiate this commitment if needed. As the appointment draws near, our office asks for a confirmation that this time works for the patient.

As part of this commitment, I will be escorting the patient to their appointment on time.

Then I will be outlining the plan to them and asking for their permission to complete this. As I listen to their response, I modify the appointment plan to honor and respect their choice. An atmosphere of honor, respect, has been set for this appointment.

The patient is more likely to allow me to deposit in their trust account if I am consistent in carrying out what we have agreed upon.

If this is a pattern that repeats itself, then the patient will begin to trust me with supporting them in meeting their dental health needs. I continue to make small deposits by being enthusiastic, cheerful, respectful, and supportive.

If I can't keep my agreement, then I must own up and ask forgiveness. The person then has the opportunity to forgive me. If I want to redeposit in the trust account, it would be a wise strategy to recompense the person in a tangible way for breaking that promise.

In that way, I acknowledge the value of our relationship. If it costs me something, I am likely to make future plans that can be delivered.

The basic building blocks for trust are outlined in this example. These include open honest communication on what I am committed to and what the other person is committed to, an agreed upon outcome, a time line for this outcome and a strategy to address an unsatisfactory outcome.

Several differing ways contribute to the level of trust that a person may bestow upon another.

Trust built upon referral

My goal is to keep my car in great running condition. Beyond driving safely, I am not qualified to take care of my car. I take my vehicle for service to a local mechanic who was recommended to me by my family. I rely on him to evaluate the different systems in my car and to let me know when I need to upgrade or repair anything. I have developed a relationship with this man and I trust him to guide my decisions in this area.

This business man began with a measure of my trust because of the recommendation of someone else's opinion of him. I first trusted this man because my family members told me about their experience of receiving good service with him. Because he was consistent with me, my trust level towards him increased.

On one occasion, this mechanic referred me to another establishment for a warranty related issue. While there, the attendant suggested further service. At my next scheduled tune-up, I told my regular mechanic about the other shop attendant's suggestion. He said that he appreciated their point, but he was confident that I could wait on this service for a time in the future. He gained another level of trust with me when he honored the other shop.

Behavior that causes costly withdrawals

Sometimes I fall into a pattern of complaining or murmuring. As I indulge myself in grousing about real or imagined inconveniences or question the motives of others, I erode both my own morale and potentially affect the morale of those around me. This has a significant negative effect on my trust account with others.

Another costly withdrawal from the trust account is to ridicule others. The other danger to a trust account is originating or repeating gossip. Someone said that gossip is many times a repetition of part of the truth told in a manner that places another in an unflattering light.

A deeper level of trust is built when one demonstrates commitment to an ethical standard that guards the other's welfare. How I treat others will eventually return to me. I commit to make it a win/win!

Application:

Think of a business or organization that has won your trust. How was that gained?

Think of an individual that you trust. What actions on this person's part contributed to that trust?

When have you lost trust in someone? What happened to erode your trust?

Can you think of a time when someone lost trust in you? What could you do to restore that trust?

How committed are you to being one that can be trusted?

What small daily changes can you make in order to establish and build a trust account with a friend or a coworker?

Book Photo credit:
7 Keys Photo Corina Rosu
Copyright:<ahref='https://www.123rf.com/profile_coramax'>coramax / 123RF Stock Photo</a>

Please rate my book.

I would be honored if you would take a few moments to rate this book on Amazon.com. If you would please rate it at 5-stars and write a short comment such as "strategies I can use" or "encouraging read", I would be very grateful! Of course, longer, enthusiastic comments are greatly appreciated as well!

Just in case you're thinking of rating this book as 3-stars or less, I kindly ask that you please not rate this book. Instead, would you please give me your direct feedback, so that I can improve it for the next edition?

I am seriously committed to over-delivering valuable content to all my readers!

Simply email your feedback to:

guardagainstburnout@gmail.com

Thank you!
Leslie Bower

www.ingramcontent.com/pod-product-compliance
Lightning Source LLC
Chambersburg PA
CBHW061231180526
45170CB00003B/1250